T0414346

A DAY IN THE LIFE OF A
MARINE BIOLOGIST

THIS EDITION

Produced for DK by WonderLab Group LLC
Jennifer Emmett, Erica Green, Kate Hale, *Founders*

Editor Maya Myers; **Photography Editor** Kelley Miller; **Managing Editor** Rachel Houghton;
Designers Project Design Company; **Researcher** Michelle Harris; **Copy Editor** Lori Merritt;
Indexer Connie Binder; **Proofreader** Susan K. Hom; **Series Reading Specialist** Dr. Jennifer Albro

First American Edition, 2025
Published in the United States by DK Publishing, a division of Penguin Random House LLC
1745 Broadway, 20th Floor, New York, NY 10019

DK books are available at special discounts when purchased in bulk for sales promotions, premiums, fund-raising,
or educational use. For details, contact:
DK Publishing Special Markets, 1745 Broadway, 20th Floor, New York, NY 10019
SpecialSales@dk.com

Printed and bound in China
Super Readers Lexile® levels 310L to 490L
Lexile® is the registered trademark of MetaMetrics, Inc. Copyright © 2024 MetaMetrics, Inc. All rights reserved.

The publisher would like to thank the following for their kind permission to reproduce their images:
a=above; c=center; b=below; l=left; r=right; t=top; b/g=background
Alamy Stock Photo: Hugh Harrop 13cla, mauritius images GmbH / Reinhard Dirscherl 8, 30tl, Nature Picture
Library / Pete Oxford 20-21t, 21b, Nature Picture Library / Sam Hobson 28, Nature Picture Library / Tony Wu 24br;
Dreamstime.com: Hotshotsworldwide 7b, Yiu Tung Lee 6cb, 30clb, Seadam 6-7 (Background), Benjawan
Sittidech 10-11 (Background), Paul Van Slooten 6cl, Tunatura 4-5, Zavgsg 11; **Getty Images:** AFP / Cris Bouroncle
26tr, AFP / Rodrigo Buendia 13cr, Boston Globe 16c, Corbis Historical / Vittoriano Rastelli 15, DigitalVision / Monty
Rakusen 9tr, Handout 29, Moment / Antonio Busiello 3, 17, 30cla, Moment / by wildestanimal 1, Alexis Rosenfeld
24cr; **Getty Images / iStock:** 33karen33 6cr, 30bl, E+ / Global_Pics 10, E+ / Ultramarinfoto 24tl; **naturepl.com:**
Stefan Christmann 14, Doug Perrine 19c, 19b; **NOAA:** 12, 22b, 27, 30cl, Sönke Johnsen and Edie Widder 23t, John
McCord UNC CSI – Battle of the Atlantic expedition 25, NOAA Fisheries / Paul Wade 22cr, NOAA Fisheries / Staci
DeSchryver 18; **Ocean Research & Conservation Association (ORCA):** 23cr; **Science Photo Library:** Oona
Stern 26bl; **U.S. Geological Survey:** William Link, Ph.D 9t, 16b

Cover images: *Front:* **Dreamstime.com:** Isselee tl, cr, Natuska (Background); **Getty Images / iStock:** E+ / Rainer
von Brandis; *Back:* **Dreamstime.com:** Tetiana Kozachok clb, Evgenii Naumov cr, VectorMine cra; *Spine:*
Dreamstime.com: Isselee, Natuska; **Getty Images / iStock:** E+ / Rainer von Brandis

www.dk.com

A DAY IN THE LIFE OF A
MARINE
BIOLOGIST

Ruth A. Musgrave

Contents

Ocean Scientists

Marine biologists study things that live in and near the ocean.

These scientists learn about animals. The animals swim, jump, fly, and float. They study ocean plants and seaweed, too.

Let's meet some marine biologists at work!

In the Ocean

Marine biologists work everywhere in the ocean. Many work far out at sea. Some dive into the water to go to work. This biologist is working in a forest made of seaweed.

These biologists work together to explore the sea. They also explore land near the ocean. Some sea animals come onto the land.

Tools for the Job

Marine biologists use special gear. A wet suit keeps them warm. They look through a mask. Swim fins help them swim.

Marine biologists take pictures. They make notes. A computer helps keep track of things they discover.

Scuba gear lets people breathe underwater.

Marine biologists live on a ship on long trips.

Let's Get to Work!

Marine biologists can go to work in small boats or on big ships. It can take many days to find the animals they study.

These marine biologists find the whales they want to study.

These marine biologists learn about sea turtles.

Study Near Shore

Some marine biologists work where it is very cold. They study penguins. It is noisy and smelly here. But the smell is worth it. They get to see these incredible chicks.

Penguins lay their eggs on land.

These marine biologists study seals.
They measure the seals.
They learn how fast baby seals grow.

This marine biologist
swims through the reef.
He looks for changes in
the coral.
Some corals are sick.
He wants to learn why.
He wants to help them
get better.

Biologists at Sea

Marine biologists go far out to sea. Some watch for seabirds. Others look for whales.

Some marine biologists look for baby fish. They learn how the fish live.

Some baby fish look different from their parents.

These marine biologists catch sharks. They lift a shark onto the ship. They put a tag on the shark's fin.

Then, they let it go.
The tag will
show them
where the
shark swims.

Tools for the Sea

Marine biologists use different tools. This drone flies above the sea. It follows whales to learn how fast they swim.

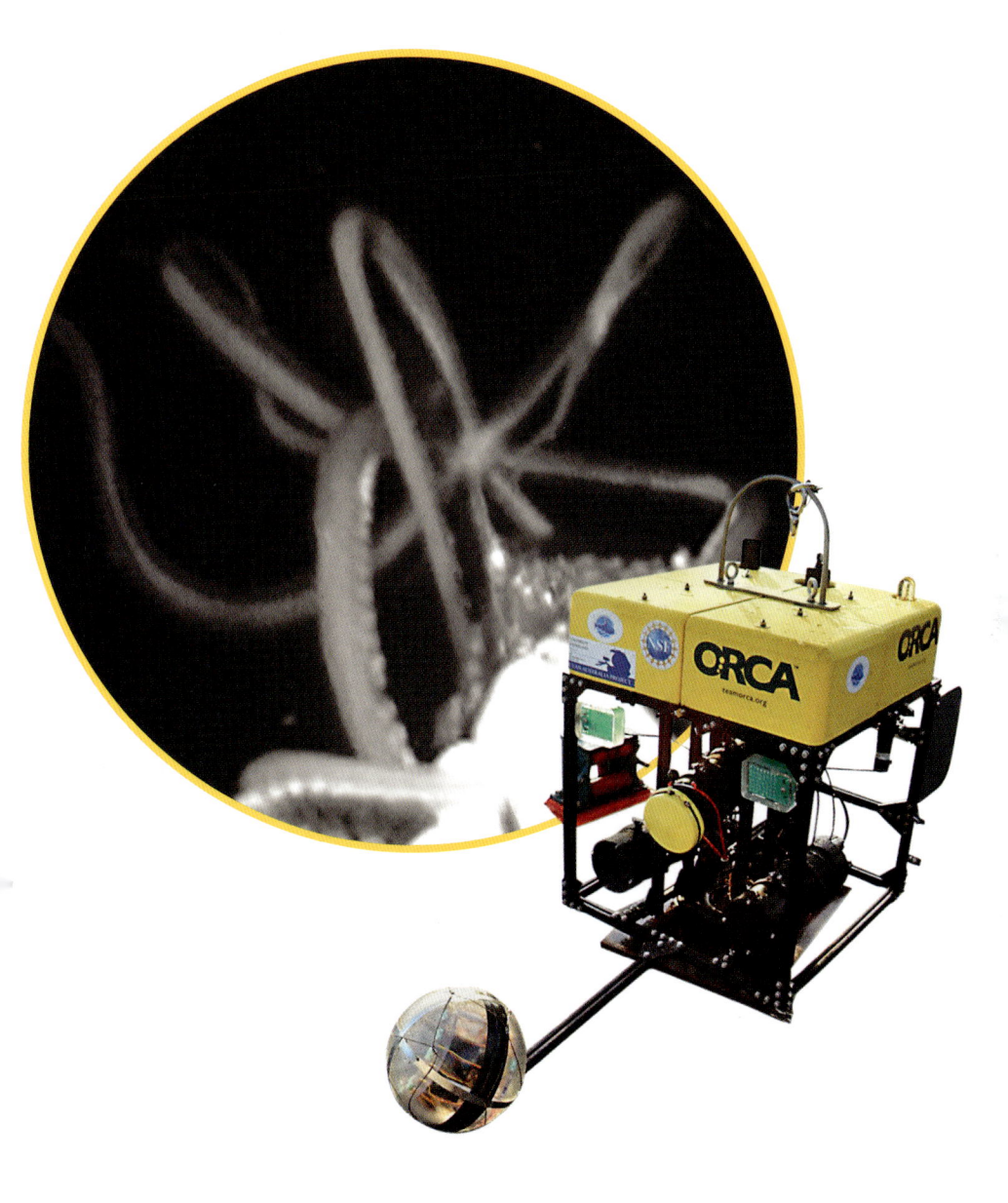

This camera takes pictures of animals in the deep sea. A giant squid swims right by.

This marine biologist uses a camera. She takes photos under the water.

This marine biologist uses a hydrophone. This is an underwater microphone. He listens to whale noises.

This marine biologist
goes into the deep sea.
He looks for new animals.

Sorting Facts

This marine biologist looks at old pictures and new pictures. He looks for ways the animals change.

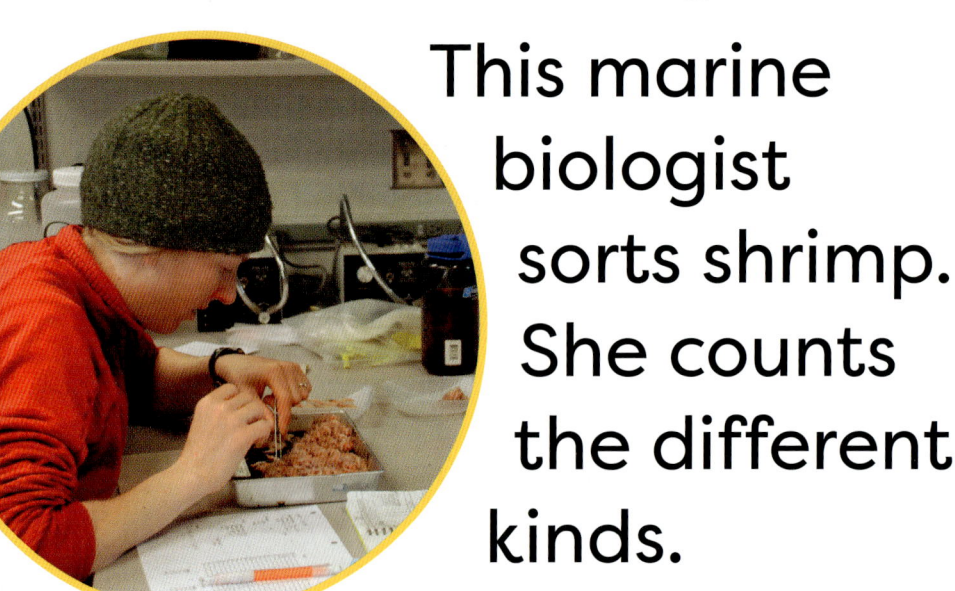

This marine biologist sorts shrimp. She counts the different kinds.

Marine biologists gather facts. They think about the facts. They write about what they learn. They share what they learn. This helps us understand the oceans.

Save the Sea

Marine biologists ask lots of questions. Then, they look for answers. Their job is important. Sea animals need our help. Trash, warmer water, and too much fishing make the ocean unhealthy.

A marine biologist freeing a bird trapped in ocean trash

A rescued otter pup

Every day, marine biologists learn something new. They help find ways to save sea life.

Glossary

biologist
a scientist who studies living things

coral
a tiny sea animal that can build rocky reefs

drone
a tool that flies and carries a camera

marine
having to do with the ocean or sea life

seabird
a bird that hunts in the sea

Index

Quiz

Answer the questions to see what you have learned. Check your answers with an adult.

1. What do marine biologists study?

2. What tool do marine biologists use to follow whales from the sky?

3. Name an animal marine biologists study in the cold.

4. Name two ways marine biologists can get to where they work.

5. Do marine biologists always work alone?

1. Things that live in the ocean 2. A drone 3. Penguins
4. Big ships and small boats 5. No, they work together.